Clark Public Library
303 Westfield Ave.
Clark, NJ 07066
(732)388-5999

FOURSQUARE AND OTHER LOCATION-BASED SERVICES

CHECKING IN, STAYING SAFE & BEING SAVVY

PHILIP WOLNY

rosen publishing's
rosen central®

New York

Published in 2012 by The Rosen Publishing Group, Inc.
29 East 21st Street, New York, NY 10010

Copyright © 2012 by The Rosen Publishing Group, Inc.

First Edition

Library of Congress Cataloging-in-Publication Data

Wolny, Philip.
Foursquare and other location-based services: checking in, staying safe & being savvy/Philip Wolny.—1st ed.
    p. cm.—(Digital and information literacy)
Includes bibliographical references and index.
ISBN 978-1-4488-5554-4 (library binding)—
ISBN 978-1-4488-5615-2 (pbk.)—
ISBN 978-1-4488-5616-9 (6-pack)
1. Online social networks—Juvenile literature. 2. Location-based services—Juvenile literature. I. Title.
HM742.W65 2012
006.7'54—dc23

                                                      2011023330

Manufactured in the United States of America

CPSIA Compliance Information: Batch #W12YA: For further information, contact Rosen Publishing, New York, New York, at 1-800-237-9932.

CONTENTS

INTRODUCTION

Imagine you and your fellow students are on a class trip heading to the Smithsonian museum and research complex in Washington, D.C. You and a couple dozen of your classmates and chaperones are going to split up into teams and cover all of the Smithsonian's nineteen museums and galleries. Your mission is to divide up the various museums you will all visit, plan each visit and document it, and organize breaks throughout the day to join back up and talk about your visits.

In the past, you might have had to equip everyone with maps of the area and hope that everyone could find their way. Nowadays, we are lucky to have technology that gives a huge helping hand. One of the most exciting new technologies that can help people on school projects and site-seeing trips like this is a location-based service. And perhaps the most well known and widely used is becoming ever more popular throughout society: Foursquare.

Chances are you've heard of Foursquare and other location-based services, such as Gowalla and Facebook's Places application, which can be used on smartphones. These applications, or apps, allow you to track your visits to many different kinds of places: stores, museums, schools, parks, restaurants, coffee shops, movie theaters, and community centers, among many

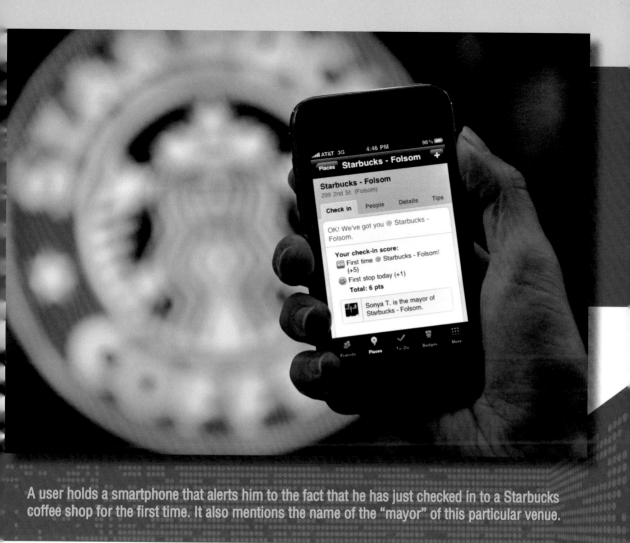

A user holds a smartphone that alerts him to the fact that he has just checked in to a Starbucks coffee shop for the first time. It also mentions the name of the "mayor" of this particular venue.

other ventures. More important, they allow you to share this information with friends and family.

Foursquare users also benefit from special deals, discounts, free give-aways, and access to information and tips that others do not. In many places, you can access information, comments, opinions, and helpful hints left by previous visitors. These can help you plan your visit better and make it more fun and informative. For example, on your Smithsonian trip, you can get Foursquare tips that tell you that one entrance to the Museum of

American History is much less crowded than another. Another tip might tell you the quickest way to get to the IMAX theater, where the best photography exhibits are, or the cheapest deals on food or gifts.

Location-based services (LBS) are made possible by linking Global Positioning System (GPS) technologies (which track a user's location) to the capabilities of the World Wide Web, along with other vital features such as instant messaging. An LBS is a mobile version of social networking sites. In addition, Foursquare and similar location-based services are taking the spirit of competition and fun typical of video games and applying them to users' social lives. We'll see exactly how such networks let users interact while engaging in friendly, good-humored competition.

As we will explore in more detail in the chapters ahead, Foursquare and other location-based social network services are changing the way we study, work, and play, and will continue to do so for years to come. Let's see how these services work and "check in" to this ever-changing world of mobile social networking!

Chapter 1

Finding Your Way in Foursquare

ince its beginnings, the Internet has been used as a social platform. However, it was only in the last decade or so that social network services, or platforms, have exploded in popularity. Beginning with networks such as Friendster, and later MySpace, and now with Facebook (currently the most popular social network), these Web sites have grown into gigantic online communities.

What Makes Social Networks "Social"?

Many social networks share some common features. Users often have a profile where they can post information, pictures, and videos. There are also usually e-mail services built in, along with instant messaging (IM). For many social networks, such as Goodreads.com for book lovers, the focus is a very specific interest shared by users: gaming, movies, sports, cars, cooking, environmentalism, and thousands of other options.

Lately, far better connectivity for mobile devices like smartphones and tablet computers like Apple's iPad have made the mobile Internet ever more

Facebook sales engineer Ankur Pansari uses his company's mobile app installed on the Google Android platform to do some social networking on the go. Facebook is an important competitor in the geosocial market that is led by Foursquare.

popular for social network applications. More people are now using such applications on mobile devices rather than on their home computers.

Dodgeball and Foursquare: The Early Years of LBS

Foursquare, as we now use it, is based on an older LBS called Dodgeball, created in 2000 by two New York University (NYU) technology students, Dennis Crowley and Alex Rainert. At that time, the service depended on users texting their location to a central number in order to receive information on whether their friends were nearby. Google acquired Dodgeball in 2005 but discontinued it in 2009, replacing it with its own LBS, Google Latitude.

Crowley later partnered with Naveen Selvadurai to create Foursquare, launching the service in March 2009. Technology for mobile devices like Apple's iPhone, Blackberrys, and other smartphones was much improved in the years since Dodgeball debuted. Now, users of smartphones and other portable devices had GPS to help them.

LBS pioneers Dennis Crowley *(left)* and Naveen Selvadurai, Foursquare's developers, attend the Made in NY Awards ceremony in New York City.

GPS is a free satellite service run by the U.S. government. It provides time and location tracking for users, helping them figure out their exact location anywhere on Earth, as long as they can connect to the signals of four GPS satellites. For years, civilian users mostly used it for finding the best travel routes from point A to point B and helping them with directions if they got lost. With the rise of social networks and better mobile devices, however, GPS could now be used for many purposes previously unimaginable.

GOWALLA AND OTHER LOCATION-BASED SERVICES

Gowalla and Other Location-Based Services

While Foursquare has become the most widely used location-based service, it is not the be-all, end-all of LBS. Another popular LBS is Gowalla, which allows users to collect "stamps" in a collection called a passport. These are akin to Foursquare's badges. You collect a stamp for each place you visit when you check in. Foursquare and Gowalla are often quite similar. For example, Foursquare has "venues," while Gowalla has "spots." Yet with Gowalla you can also "pick up" virtual items, taking them to other spots. Each of these virtual items has a history associated with it bestowed by previous users. In addition, Gowalla lets users connect several visits to spots into larger "trips."

The emphasis with Foursquare is alerting one's friends to one's current location and inviting them to join you there. With Gowalla, this aspect is less important. Gathering experiences, much like a tourist might do on vacation, is emphasized more.

Finally, while Foursquare features GPS technology, it can still be used without it, while Gowalla cannot. In addition, Gowalla checks you in to specific locations anywhere on Earth's surface, while Foursquare works solely with established addresses.

What You Need

To use services like Foursquare, you need a smartphone or other GPS- and Internet-enabled mobile device, like an Apple iPad. A smartphone is perhaps the most convenient mobile device for use with Foursquare. Currently, the three most widely used are Apple's iPhone, the Blackberry, and Android-powered devices. Other phones include the Palm, Ovi, and Windows Phone.

Once you have signed up as a Foursquare member and downloaded and installed the application to your phone, you can link your Foursquare account to other networks you belong to and/or to your e-mail. For example, it's relatively easy to connect to Facebook, Twitter, and other applications. Combining geographical location ("geolocation") and social networking, Foursquare and similar applications are sometimes referred to as geosocial networks.

Checking In and Giving Tips

Arriving at a location and using Foursquare is called "checking in." You can check in to nearly any location imaginable: a café; a museum; a clothing or other retail store; a sports venue; a restaurant; your own school cafeteria, library, gymnasium, or auditorium; and many more places.

Once you check in to a place, any friends of yours who are nearby using Foursquare will be informed via a status update that you are there. They can then make plans to come join you or meet you at another nearby location. If you are trying to meet someone at the local bookstore (your friend Maria, for example) you might read, "Maria has checked in to Anytown Books," or a similar message received via your Facebook or Foursquare feed.

But simply checking in, while fun, is just the beginning. One of the points of checking in is to leave "tips"—information, reviews, and opinions about the venue, whether good or bad. Maria might leave a tip that the coffee is good at this bookstore, that a new book just came out from a favorite

Already a member? Login

Find places, people, tags   SEARCH

CHECK-IN
FIND YOUR FRIENDS
UNLOCK YOUR CITY

Foursquare on your phone gives you & your friends new ways of exploring
your city. Earn points & unlock badges for discovering new things. LEARN MORE

JOIN NOW

RECENT ACTIVITY

 Kenny H. in Culver City, CA:
unlocked the 'Superstar' badge.

 Seth G. in New York, NY:
became the mayor of Esca.

 Geoffrey R. in Sherbrooke, QC:
unlocked the 'Explorer' badge.

 Derk R. in Hengelo, Overijssel:
became the mayor of Creatieve Fabriek.

 Justin D. in Atlanta, GA:
became the mayor of Gill's Alterations.

 Yvonne S. in Stuttgart, Baden-Württemberg:
became the mayor of Stuttgarter Volksbank.

 Jessica L. in Astoria, NY:
became the mayor of JILFs Winery.

 Tyler E. in Pensacola, FL:
unlocked the 'I'm on a boat!' badge.

GET IT NOW

iPhone →

BlackBerry →

ANDROID →

palm →

OTHER DEVICES →

DEVELOPERS:
USE OUR API TO BUILD
YOUR OWN APPS
find out how →

BUSINESSES:
USE FOURSQUARE TO
REWARD YOUR CUSTOMERS
find out how →

FOLLOW US ON

twitter tumblr.

This sample Foursquare feed (https://foursquare.com) shows how users can view and track the
various recent activities of their contacts, whether they are unlocking badges, becoming
mayors, or checking in to venues.

author, or that there's a sale under way. Leaving details about a venue allows other Foursquare users to decide whether to visit that venue or not and get the most out of their experience

The same process works in reverse: your friends who visited a venue first can help you get the most out of your visit there or can warn you away from an experience you won't enjoy. You can also see the tips posted by any other users who have visited that venue, not just those of your friends.

Badges and More Badges

Just as Boy and Girl Scouts earn badges for learning something or mastering a skill, Foursquare lets you earn "badges" when you check in to new places. The more places you visit using Foursquare, the higher the rank of badge you will earn.

If you have just started using Foursquare, you will earn the "Newbie" badge with your first check-in. If you're in an area that contains many Foursquare venues, or have friends who use it who can point you in the right direction, you can prob- ably gain newbie status pretty quickly. Once you check in to ten different venues, you gain the "Adventurer" badge, followed by "Explorer" (twenty-five venues), and "Superstar" (fifty venues).

Naveen Selvadurai, cofounder of Foursquare, discusses the LBS's badge system at the Seoul Digital Forum in South Korea.

Adding Venues

An important feature of Foursquare is the ability to check in to a new place that no other user has ever visited and add it as a venue. If you want to add a venue, first make sure it's not already listed. Once you're sure no Foursquare user has visited and added the venue before, you can add it. However, as the Foursquare Web site advises, "Add the place if it's an actual venue where people would check in, and one you want to be visible in a public search."

Do not add venues that should really remain private, or that you would need permission to add, like a friend's house. Only those places that are open to the general public and of interest to many people—not just your small circle of friends and family—should be added. Use your best judgment, or ask someone (a parent, teacher, or other responsible adult) if you're unsure whether or not to add a location as a venue.

Chapter 2

Foursquare at School

Students can be just as social in the school environment as they are in their private lives. Most teens' closest friends are from school. Plus, classmates often have to work together on school projects, in after-school clubs, or for school-related fund-raisers, events, productions, performances, or other activities. Foursquare can help facilitate all of these group activities, helping students to work and learn together and forge stronger and more positive social ties among each other.

Teachers can get in on the game, too. As stated in the Introduction, Foursquare can add extra dimensions of education and entertainment to field trips and other school-related excursions. Educational or historical venues can be assigned as destinations that need to be visited to complete a project, perform research, or gather objects in a class scavenger hunt.

Putting the "Extra" in "Extracurricular"

To drum up school spirit, few things help like being a member of or supporting a school team. Whether cheering on your school team or engaging in friendly rivalries with competing teams, Foursquare can be a fun way to connect.

A volleyball player checks in to her school gymnasium via Foursquare on her smartphone. Athletes, performers, and their fans and audience members can all benefit from the school-based use of geosocial networks.

If, for example, you are on the baseball team and are playing an away game on the other side of town, you can see if the baseball field where you will be playing has been added as a Foursquare venue. If not, adding it and alerting your network of friends—in this case, your classmates, players' parents, and fans—can help drum up a good crowd.

If you are involved in drama, choir, orchestra, the glee club, or another type of performing art, you can use Foursquare in much the same way. Add your school auditorium as a venue and post information about the production and its showtimes. In this way, friends, schoolmates, and even parents and teachers who might be in your Foursquare network can be encouraged to attend. They may get the word out to an even wider network of possible audience members. With Foursquare, people never have to be out of the loop anymore, missing events they would have liked to attend or having important scheduled activities slip their minds.

Running for "Mayor"

With Foursquare, the main competition is seeing who can visit the most venues, especially on a regular basis. If you check in to a venue on more days in a month than any other user, you will officially be dubbed "mayor" of that venue. One thing to remember is that you need to have a profile picture for your Foursquare account before you can do many things, including becoming mayor. Photos have to be two hundred kilobytes or smaller, in .jpg, .gif, or .png formats. You also need to have checked the setting "Participate in Foursquare Mayorships."

When checking in to a venue, remember to use the "Share with friends?" tab marked "Yes." If you check in privately, or "off the grid," the check-in will count toward your mayorship but will not "unlock" the mayorship. You can also take advantage of the feature that lets you know if you are within ten check-ins of being declared mayor. This feature informs users how many days are left before he or she is crowned mayor.

How might mayorships work in your school life? Imagine your teacher assigns you a project in which you have to spend a certain amount of time at the school computer lab. The person who becomes mayor of the computer lab might earn special privileges or prizes from the teacher or school for his or her hard work and dedication to the project. Perhaps you're on a sports team. If you become mayor of the school gym, athletic field, or swimming pool, you can impress your coach or physical education teacher with how often you are working out.

Foursquare Has an Important Announcement!

Another possible use of Foursquare is to have students, faculty, and staff work together to add venues in and around the school that will assist students in their activities in various ways. If you are having a school election,

School events can be enriched and enhanced by using Foursquare or other networks to inform, entertain, and empower students to participate more fully in academic and extracurricular activities.

for example, the school gym, auditorium, and other ballot box locations can be added as venues. Foursquare users can then check in and get reminders that they should vote or be provided with vital information about the issues involved in the elections and the candidates' positions on them.

The office, school library, or other destinations might be where you have to register for events or pick up other things like school athletic jackets or uniforms, class rings, yearbooks, and other items. In today's busy world, we often need reminders, and the tips and information we share via location-based networks can work to our benefit. Receiving a tip like "Remember to drop off your completed yearbook order form at the school office" or "Physical exams for the fall athletic season will be held at the nurse's office on Friday at 3:30 PM" can mean the difference between getting something done on time or missing the boat entirely.

Foursquare Goes to College

Foursquare was introduced to Western Kentucky University (WKU) in early 2011. WKU added one hundred campus venues to Foursquare. University officials worked with campus catering and other stores to provide incentives for students to use the location-based service, including discounts and freebies. Ultimately, WKU and other schools have found that badges and other perks have helped students explore their campuses more thoroughly and increased participation in university and campus activities.

Foursquare: Big Man on Campus

As part of its "Foursquare for Universities" initiative, Foursquare's Web site lists several ways that its network might be useful to high school and college students. One way is inspiring students to explore their school facilities and campus and encourage them to get involved in campus events and activities. Another is by leaving geolocation-based tips and information relating to the campus that informs students about their school's traditions and history. In addition, school educators and administrators can use the platform as a guide to campus facilities. In grade or high school, this might be a simple matter of helping students (especially new students) easily find the principal's office, classrooms, the auditorium, gym, the lunchroom, the nurse's office, and bathrooms and locker rooms.

For college students, where the campus is usually much larger than a high school's and its facilities more numerous and far-flung, new students might feel a little less lost and bewildered if they are equipped with Foursquare. With all of the important venues available to them on campus, along with people's tips and bits of information about them, new students

Foursquare and other LBS can help new students get their bearings in an unfamiliar school and a new town.

may feel more confident, at home, and "in the know." Think about how much easier a college campus might be to navigate if your smartphone tells you where the dining halls, dorms, campus bookstore, libraries, lecture halls, and computer labs are.

Another obvious, but clever, way schools are using the service is by letting students unlock various badges, all specific to school life itself, reports Jodie O'Dell in a January 2011 article on Mashable.com. For example, you might have a "Bookworm Bender" badge if you hit the library or study area after classes or a "Munchies" badge for five check-ins to campus eateries. The "Smells Like School Spirit" badge could be unlocked with five visits to a school sports venue, while an "Explorer" badge might be awarded for check-ins to ten different school campus locations.

Chapter 3

Foursquare Around Town

When you are growing up, you gain experiences, confidence, and skills that help ease you into adult life. School is not the only place, of course, that you learn these things. Increasingly, much human interaction and communication is occurring online, and experiences are shared through digital media. It is becoming the norm to interact with others via digital social networks, so it's a good idea to become familiar with them. While they will never and can never be a substitute for actual face-to-face communication, they are rapidly becoming a useful, everyday tool for people to stay in touch, make new connections, and find out about what is going on around town.

Foursquare Partners Up

Foursquare is not just a fun new way to broadcast one's location to friends, comment upon one's activities and the venues they take place in, and compete over badges and mayorships. In fact, you may notice that more and more businesses near you are building partnerships with Foursquare. One

This Foursquare user is offered a free dessert for checking in to the café. Many venues are increasingly offering discounts and free giveaways for users of LBS networks.

obvious reason is that people competing to check in to a place will often become customers, if that place is selling goods or services. Thus, both independently owned businesses and huge chains, from the neighborhood dry cleaner to Starbucks, are getting in on the action. How do these partnerships work?

In some places, you can receive free products or discounts if you become the mayor of a venue. If you go to a gym ten times, for example, you might get a "Gym Rat" badge. But if you become mayor, you might get free energy drinks, win a private class, or earn free gym equipment or new training gear. According to *Time*'s January 2010 article on Foursquare, different businesses have different criteria for rewards. Based in Boulder, Colorado, Modmarket eatery offers free pizza to anyone who checks in ten times and a free drink to the current mayor. Some carwashes are offering $2 off when drivers check in using Foursquare.

Many different businesses, local and national, are partnering with Foursquare. Zagat Survey, a publisher of international restaurant and enter-tainment guides, has enabled its readers to check in to the thousands of restaurants it lists in its guidebooks. Frequent visitors can earn a "Foodie" badge. Zagat even created a blog site that it calls "Meet the Mayor," where it interviews a randomly selected Foursquare mayor of one of the establish-ments covered in its guides.

Checking In to Your Community

Getting together with friends who also use Foursquare can be a great way to learn about your community. You might even try creating your own games and activities, using check-ins, tips, and instant messaging to make them even more fun.

If you have ever been on a scavenger hunt, you know it can be an exciting game. You might create a Foursquare-based game that uses your entire town or neighborhood as a sort of game board. Two or more teams can play, with one team leaving clues via tips and instant messaging. Pick five to ten unnamed locations or venues, and create clues to help the other team identify, locate, and check in to them. You may also require that certain pieces of information be retrieved or inexpensive objects be purchased from the venues. These may include the first sentence of Jane Austen's *Emma* from the public library, a cell phone photo of a certain painting hanging in the art museum, a book of stamps from the post office, a cupcake from the new bakery, and pamphlets from the local historical society.

File   Edit   View   Favorites   Tools   Help

FOURSQUARE ON THE RUN

Foursquare on the Run

Foursquare can be used in many aspects of daily life, and countless software companies are coming up with new ways to boost its utility. For example, a company based in Boston, Massachusetts, called FitnessKeeper creates social networking apps for people interested in physical fitness. Its Runkeeper app uses Foursquare to award performance-based badges.

Using the GPS system most smartphones have, you can earn Foursquare badges through FitnessKeeper while walking, running, or cycling. Badges you can unlock or earn include a "Warm Up" badge (any three activities, like running, biking, and walking, with a distance greater than 0.6 miles or 1 kilometer), a 5K badge (5 kilometer, or 3 mile badge), a 26.2 badge if you run a marathon (26.2 miles or 42 km). There is even an "Over Achiever" badge if you complete five different kinds of physical activity—such as hiking, biking, running, skiing, walking—on three different days.

Social Networks Go Geosocial

It seemed only natural that once location-based services like Foursquare appeared they would integrate with existing social networking services like Facebook and Twitter. Nowadays, many people are active on all three, to the point that it may be difficult to remember which platform or service first alerted you to a bit of news or about an event you want to attend.

As a result, Facebook quickly recognized Foursquare as a possible competitor, and it hoped to make money in the same geosocial market. In mid-2010, Facebook launched Facebook Places, a similar geosocial network to

Even in the heat of a competition, athletes can geosocialize and use LBS to maximize their performance. Here, a runner promotes the Runkeeper app.

Foursquare. It later added Facebook Deals as a subset of the Places application. While Facebook Places has gained in popularity, Foursquare continues to grow steadily and has many loyal users.

The Facebook Places app broadcasts your check-in to the Place page, on your friends' news feeds, and on your profile, or wall. Just as you may tag your friends in a photo, you can also tag your friends in a check-in, so that they appear in the update even if they are not on Facebook Places. A "Here Now" feature alerts you and your friends when you are both checked in to the same place. You can also browse the status updates of friends checked in nearby. The "Deals" feature is similar to Foursquare's deal offerings as well, in that it provides users with discounts and free items for visiting particular sites repeatedly.

The popular microblogging site Twitter has also jumped on the geo-social bandwagon, launching its Twitter Places application in June 2010. Using Twitter's site or your own smartphone to broadcast your Twitter message, or tweet, you can also click on Foursquare venues to view other tweets linked to those locations. At the same time, you can tag your location with your tweets. In addition, Twitter has partnered with Gowalla, another location-based service, to give the same capabilities to its users.

This integration of location-based and social networking services can benefit you if you're seeking information about a locality, going shopping, doing research, trying to meet up with friends, or simply looking for something fun to do. Foursquare can thus make average, familiar places you are used to (your school, town center, shopping mall, pizza parlor) more interesting, infusing them with a certain mystery and sense of exploration and discovery. It can also make unfamiliar places easier to successfully and pleasurably navigate. These geosocial networks can be tools for encouraging our friends, neighbors, classmates, siblings, and parents to try new and exciting activities and to visit new places.

TEN GREAT QUESTIONS
TO ASK AN IT SPECIALIST

1   How can I prevent competition for mayorships from getting out of hand?

2   What sorts of places and venues are appropriate to add to Foursquare?

3   What sort of places and venues are appropriate for teens to check in to via Foursquare?

4   How can I increase my privacy by altering my default settings on Foursquare?

5   How can I go "off-the-grid" on Foursquare?

6   When I'm "off-the-grid," can selected friends still receive my tips, posts, and status updates?

7   When I'm "off-the-grid," can I still collect badges and compete for and win mayorships?

8   How do other location-based services differ from Foursquare? Are there any that are more teen- or school-oriented?

9   How can my school and teachers use Foursquare to enhance activities, lessons, and projects?

10   What are the dangers of using Foursquare? Have there been any crimes related to the use of location-based services?

Chapter 4

Checking In and Checking Yourself

As social networks like Foursquare and Facebook become ever more important in our lives, it is essential to police ourselves and our words and actions and to do everything possible to ensure our safety and that of our fellow users. Some of the common perils users of location-based and social network services face are bullying, harassment, and social exclusion; excessive self-exposure and oversharing; loss of privacy; and increased vulnerability to cyberstalking and other criminal activity.

Cyberbullying

Just as bullying, taunting, harassing, and excluding others in person is wrong, so, too, is such antisocial behavior unacceptable online. We now live much of our lives on Facebook, Twitter, Foursquare, and within other "wired" communities. Bad behavior is just as destructive and hurtful in the virtual world as it is in the actual world.

Every school or neighborhood has some kids who may not quite fit in. Insecure bullies often target these "outsiders" to boost their own fragile

Whether dealing with cyberbullies, predators, or thieves, it pays to always remain vigilant, wary, and extremely cautious when using social networks, including location-based ones.

social standing. When this kind of harassment occurs on sites like Facebook or Foursquare, it's still bullying. The anonymity of digital communication does not make bullying and harassment OK. In fact, it's even more cowardly to hide behind the invisibility of digital communication to victimize an innocent person. Bullying and harassment can take many forms on location-based services. A group of friends may check in to a venue and then exclude one particular person. Someone may leave tips and messages that insult or make fun of someone else. A user may lure a fellow student to a certain location with the promise of meeting him or her there, and then stand them up and perhaps leave them vulnerable in a dangerous or unfamiliar part of town.

In addition, it should always be remembered that competing to be the mayor of a venue or to receive prizes, discounts, and other benefits is, in the end, only a game. It is not a life-or-death matter to be fought over. Do not let the heat of the contest get to you so much that you become angry, frustrated, bitter, or physically or verbally aggressive and violent.

Overexposed: Too Much Checking In

Just as someone can reveal too much on a blog, their Facebook profile, in a chat room, or on any number of other social networking and Web sites, the same goes for Foursquare, Gowalla, and similar location-based services. Be careful about the information you leave along with your tips. Even if you keep your friends list secure, do not post identifying information in either your profile or posts. Identifying information includes your full name, address, telephone number, school name and location, e-mail address, and Social Security number.

Also, remember to be selective about whom you agree to friend on a network like Foursquare. While it is never advisable to make friends with strangers online, it is an even worse idea to do it through a service that is designed to alert other users to your exact location in real time. Revealing personal information, especially your physical location, to strangers or acquaintances you don't trust or know well is never a good idea. When online, people can pretend to be anyone and gain your trust through deceit. Never agree to meet a stranger you have "friended" through a location-based, social networking, or other-Web-based service. It's also always a good idea to use Foursquare to broadcast your location only when you are with other friends or family members, not when you are alone.

File   Edit   View   Favorites   Tools   Help

SOCIAL NETWORKS AND CRIME

Social Networks and Crime

In February 2011, the University of Massachusetts-Dartmouth newspaper the *Torch* speculated about the possibility that social networks were putting their users in danger. While news of Foursquare-inspired crimes has not hit mainstream media, broadcasting your whereabouts to the world can indeed be dangerous. You might want to think twice about checking in to the local ice cream parlor and telling everyone you know that the whole family is with you. You never know who might take advantage of such information to attempt a burglary or other crime at your home because they know no one is there. Campus police officer Kristin Costa told the *Torch* that users of location-based and social network services should ask themselves some important and possibly life-saving questions: "Do I really know the people I've friended? Do I really trust these 'friends' with private and personal details regarding my daily routines, weekend plans, and current or future location?"

Going "Off-the-Grid"

Even among your good friends, you may not always want people to know where you are at any given hour of the day. There may be times you want to relax and enjoy a peaceful, quiet moment and may want to be out of touch and not reachable. Foursquare has numerous customizable settings that can adjust just how much exposure you have to your network of friends and how much exposure they have to you. Foursquare's Web site includes a handy chart that instructs users on how to manage check-ins and how to boost one's privacy when necessary or desired.

If you show up alone to a venue, do not broadcast your presence or the fact that no one is with you. Instead, check in "off-the-grid." It's a good idea to use Foursquare and other LBS only when you are with a group of people you know and trust.

With Foursquare, there are several settings and tabs through which you can control the location and time of your check-ins. As the default setting, your time and location for check-ins is visible to your Foursquare friends via the Friends tab and on the Web site's homepage. Users who are not part of your friend network (referred to by Foursquare as "the public") cannot see your settings.

You may notice a feature on Foursquare called "Who's Here?" If you check in at a venue, you are automatically put on a list of people at that venue that anyone can see. There are ways in which this check-in information might be abused by others. For example, a girl might check in to a coffee shop and be the only female who appears on the Foursquare list for check-ins at that location. Other users might notice and potentially harass the girl because they now know her name, some limited profile information, and the fact that she is the only female Foursquare user at that venue.

User privacy and security can often be increased by checking in "off the grid." Your check-in will not show up at all to your friends, but it will be visible to you in your app and in your private Foursquare check-in history. You will not be listed in the "Who's Here" list at a venue either. "Off the grid" check-ins can't be published to Twitter or Facebook. In addition, you should explore Foursquare's FAQ section, user blogs, and help features. These will give pointers on how to limit who can view what badges you have, your check-ins, your profile photo, which friends you connect with or not, and other private and identifying information. Most privacy settings are accessible via the User Settings tab. To view Foursquare's chart of all its privacy enhancing options, visit https://foursquare.com/privacy/grid.

Just as you may not text or call a certain friend back immediately but instead wait to respond until a more convenient time, it's perfectly fine to go off the grid sometimes. In addition, do not feel obligated to respond to messages sent from users unknown to you. Not everyone at a venue is your friend, and not everyone might have the best intentions. As with anything you do in public, be aware of your surroundings and very cautious about what information you are sending out electronically.

How Location-Based Services Can Keep You Safe

While the perils of Foursquare and other LBS apps are indeed real, the technologies involved can also be very useful in protecting the safety and security of users. The GPS feature helps prevent getting lost or will lead you to familiar territory should you become confused and "turned around." The geolocation information that Foursquare reveals to the outside world can actually save you and speed the arrival of help during an emergency.

If something unexpected happens—like car trouble—and you don't make it home for curfew, your parents and the police might be able to easily determine your location or at least your last known whereabouts. They will discover that you might be stuck halfway home with a flat tire and be relieved to know that you haven't been abducted or gotten into some other kind of danger. They will know exactly where to find you and pick you up.

MYTH Being part of a location-based service automatically puts you in harm's way and exposes you to stalkers and predators.

FACT There is very little documentation concerning people being harmed by others due to their use of Foursquare or similar location-based services. Still, it is best to use common sense and street smarts and not reveal your whereabouts to others unless you know them well. Do not post personal and identifying information, and never agree to meet a stranger who has communicated to you via a location-based or social network service.

MYTH You can use Foursquare and similar location-based services only with a smartphone.

FACT You can check in to a venue via computer or by texting to the number 50500. However, smartphones are the easiest and most convenient way to use location-based services.

MYTH Adding yet another social network to one's life is just too time-consuming, complicated, and redundant.

FACT Foursquare and other location-based services are easy to use and work ever more seamlessly with other social networks. They can and should be used in moderation, so you can enjoy "disconnected" time as well. But geosocial services like Foursquare offer a range of activities, personal interactions, explorations, and discoveries out in "the real world" that other social networks do not. This sets them apart and makes them a potentially healthier, more rewarding, more educational, and more enriching social network experience.

Many Happy Check-Ins!

Doing anything in excess is a bad idea, including spending too much time using Foursquare and other location-based services. You should always strive to balance time spent on the computer and mobile devices with school work, leisure activities, family life, time with friends, and other aspects of offline life. Yet if you use location-based services wisely, they can enhance your life and help you grow and develop.

Getting rewards for positive things like visiting museums, libraries, performing arts venues, local historical and cultural sites, and other locations that reflect your academic and personal interests can be great learning experiences and can help you bond with like-minded friends. Foursquare

With LBS networks ever expanding, you and your friends can use them to enhance your school life, shop for deals, discover all the nooks and crannies of your town, explore your interests, stay in close touch with family members, and forge closer bonds of friendship and camaraderie with an expanding circle of peers.

and similar networks let you do things in a real-time, group setting and help you build relationships.

With Foursquare and other location-based services, you can discover whole new worlds right in your own town, bond with friends, and more fully experience all that your community and the larger world have to offer. Plus, Foursquare and other geosocial networks are constantly changing, updating their services, improving their privacy controls, and partnering with various businesses and institutions to enhance your experience. It seems as if Foursquare and its LBS "cousins" will soon have everyone "checking in" and checking out the entire world in all its dazzling variety and infinite possibilities.

GLOSSARY

badge An indicator that you have achieved a certain milestone while using Foursquare; for example, checking in to a certain place a certain number of times.

check in To announce your presence or arrival at a location via a location-based service.

cyberbullying Bullying someone online, with threats or other harassment performed through chat rooms, social networks, instant messaging, blogs, e-mail, and other Web sites where young people connect and interact.

geosocial Refers to online communities or networks that combine a social aspect with a geographical, or location-based, dimension.

Global Positioning System (GPS) A free U.S. government service that enables people to utilize satellite signals to track their exact location anywhere on Earth.

location-based service (LBS) A social network based on sharing one's location with other users in real time.

mayor The title given to a Foursquare user who has checked in to a venue more than any user within a thirty-day period; "mayorship" gives users special privileges, such as free goods or services or discounted items for purchase.

off-the-grid Refers to activity conducted on Foursquare that you choose not to reveal to certain users.

smartphone A device that combines the normal functions of a mobile phone with Internet connectivity; examples include the iPhone and Blackberry devices.

social network An online community in which members set up personal profiles and communicate with friends.

tip A comment or piece of information left by other users at venues that any user can then read; e.g., at a restaurant, a user can leave a tip such as "Try the carrot cake!"

tweets Updates or messages of 140 characters or less sent via the popular Twitter application.

Twitter A popular social networking application in which users broadcast messages of no more than 140 characters to their "followers" (other users who join someone's Twitter feed and receive that person's tweets).

unlock To earn a badge or mayorship through Foursquare.

venue A physical location or site that can be added to Foursquare by a user. That venue can then be checked in to and commented upon by other users.

FOR MORE INFORMATION

Canadian Internet Project (CIP)
Ryerson University School of Radio and Television Arts
Toronto, ON M5B 2K3
Canada
(416) 979-5000, ext.7549
Web site: http://www.canadianinternetproject.ca/en/intro.htm
The CIP is a Ryerson University–based, long-running research project center-
    ing on Internet usage, trends, attitudes, and many other factors in our
    relationship with the Web.

Computer History Museum
1401 North Shoreline Boulevard
Mountain View, CA 94043
(650) 810-1010
Web site: http://www.computerhistory.org
The Computer History Museum is dedicated to exploring the development of
    computer technology from the twentieth century to the Internet age.

Family Online Safety Institute
815 Connecticut Avenue, Suite 220
Washington, DC 20006
(202) 572-6252
Web site: http://www.fosi.org
The Family Online Safety Institute is an international, nonprofit organization
    that works to develop a safer Internet for children and families. It works
    to influence public policies and educate the public.

Get Net Wise
Internet Education Foundation

1634 I Street NW
Washington, DC 20009
Web site: http://www.getnetwise.org
Get Net Wise is part of the Internet Education Foundation, which works to
    provide a safe online environment for children and families.

Internet Keep Safe Coalition
1401 K Street NW, Suite 600
Washington, DC 20005
(866) 794-7233
Web site: http://www.ikeepsafe.org
The Internet Keep Safe Coalition is an educational resource for children and
    families that educates about Internet safety and ethics associated with
    Internet technologies.

Internet Studies Department
Brandeis University
415 South Street
Waltham, MA 02453
(781) 736-2000
Web site: http://www.brandeis.edu/programs/inet
Brandeis University's Internet Studies Program offers coursework and orga-
    nizes scholarly conferences on the technological, legal, and social
    aspects of the Internet in our lives.

i-SAFE Inc.
5900 Pasteur Court, Suite 100
Carlsbad, CA 92008
(760) 603-7911
Web site: http://www.isafe.org
Founded in 1998, i-SAFE Inc. is the leader in Internet safety education.
    Available in all fifty states, Washington, D.C., and Department
    of Defense schools located across the world, i-SAFE is a nonprofit

foundation whose mission is to educate and empower youth to make their Internet experiences safe and responsible. The goal is to educate students on how to avoid dangerous, inappropriate, or unlawful online behavior.

NetSmartz
Charles B. Wang International Children's Building
699 Prince Street
Alexandria, VA 22314-3175
(800) 843-5678
Web site: http://www.netsmartz.org
NetSmartz provides children, teens, and parents with resources to help educate young people about how to surf the Internet safely.

Office of the Privacy Commissioner of Canada
112 Kent Street
Place de Ville, Tower B, 3rd Floor
Ottawa, ON K1A 1H3
Canada
Web site: http://www.priv.gc.ca/information/social/index_e.cfm
Canada's Privacy Commissioner provides resources for investigating privacy abuses and for researching privacy issues, especially those related to the recent explosion of online communities.

Pew Internet & American Life Project
Pew Research Center
1615 L Street NW, Suite 700
Washington, DC 20036
(202) 419-4300
Web site: http://www.pewinternet.org
The Pew Research Center conducts research and issues reports on many aspects of American society, including the impact of the Internet upon the individual, the citizenry, and civil society.

41

Syracuse University's School of Information Studies (iSchool)
343 Hinds Hall
Syracuse, NY 13244-4100
(315) 443-2911
Web site: http://ischool.syr.edu
Syracuse University's School of Information Studies is geared toward edu-
    cating students in every aspect of life and work in the modern digital
    society.

Web Sites

Due to the changing nature of Internet links, Rosen Publishing has developed
an online list of Web sites related to the subject of this book. This site is
updated regularly. Please use this link to access the list:

http://www.rosenlinks.com/dil/four

FOR FURTHER READING

Cindrich, Sharon, and Ali Douglass. *A Smart Girl's Guide to the Internet: How to Connect with Friends, Find What You Need, and Stay Safe Online* (American Girl Library). Middleton, WI: American Girl Publishing, 2009.

Espejo, Roman. *Does the Internet Increase Crime?* (At Issue). North Mankato, MN: Greenhaven Press, 2010.

Hile, Lori. *Social Networks and Blogs* (Mastering Media). Chicago, IL: Heinemann Raintree, 2010.

Hillstrom, Laurie. *Online Social Networks* (Technology 360). Farmington Hills, MI: Lucent/Gale, 2010.

Hussey, Tris. *Sams Teach Yourself Foursquare in 10 Minutes*. Indianapolis, IN: Sams Publishing, 2011.

Jacobs, Thomas A. *Teen Cyberbullying Investigated: Where Do Your Rights End and Consequences Begin?* Minneapolis, MN: Free Spirit Publishing, 2010.

Kiesbye, Stefan. *Are Social Networking Sites Harmful?* (At Issue). Farmington Hills, MI: Greenhaven Press, 2011.

Kuhn, Betsy. *Privacy in the Twenty-First Century*. Breckenridge, CO: Twenty-First Century Books, 2007.

Ryan, Peter K. *Social Networking* (Digital and Information Literacy). New York, NY: Rosen Central, 2011.

Waters, John K. *The Everything Guide to Social Media: All You Need to Know About Participating in Today's Most Popular Online Communities*. Avon, MA: Adams Media, 2010.

Watkins, Heidi. *Social Networking* (Issues That Concern You). Farmington Hills, MI: Greenhaven Press, 2011.

Wilkinson, Colin. *Twitter and Microblogging: Instant Communication with 140 Characters or Less* (Digital and Information Literacy). New York, NY: Rosen Central, 2012.

BIBLIOGRAPHY

Bishop, Scott. *Marketing Your Business with Foursquare*. Upper Saddle River, NJ: FT Press, 2010.

Brusilovsky, Daniel. "Are Groupon and Foursquare Meant for Each Other?" Teens in Tech, December 4, 2010. Retrieved March 2011 (http://teensintech.com/2010/12/are-foursquare-and-groupon-meant-for-each-other).

Bussgang, Jeff. "Why Did Foursquare Succeed Where Other Location-Based Services Failed?" *Business Insider*, March 2, 2011. Retrieved March 2011 (http://www.businessinsider.com/figuring-out-foursquare-2011-3).

Fletcher, Dan. "Foursquare's Twist on Facebook: A Reward for Checking In." *Time*, January 15, 2010. Retrieved April 2011 (http://www.time.com/time/business/article/0,8599,1952980,00.html).

Fletcher, Dan. "Foursquare: Where Are Location Sites Taking Us?" *Time*, September 18, 2010. Retrieved March 2011 (http://www.time.com/time/magazine/article/0,9171,2013844,00.html).

Foursquare.com. "Foursquare House Rules." Retrieved April 2011 (http://support.foursquare.com/entries/386768-foursquare-house-rules).

Judd, Jeff, ed. *Foursquare How To Boot Camp: The Fast and Easy Way to Learn the Basics with World Class Experts and Proven Tactics, Techniques, Facts, Hints, Tips, and Advice*. Ruislip, England: Tebbo, 2010.

McCarthy, Caroline. "Facebook to Foursquare: You're Out." CNet News, November 3, 2010. Retrieved March 2011 (http://news.cnet.com/8301-13577_3-20021697-36.html).

Nolan, Lynnette. "Foursquare: Is Social Media Putting Users in Danger?" University of Massachusetts-Dartmouth *Torch*, February 23, 2011. Retrieved March 2011 (http://www.umasstorch.com/index.php?option=com_content&view=article&id=480:foursquare-is-social-media-putting-users-in-danger&catid=1:front-page-news&Itemid=122).

Nosowitz, Dan. "Twitter Finally Going 'Places,' Adds Foursquare and
    Gowalla Integration Starting Today." Fast Company, June 14, 2010.
    Retrieved March 2011 (http://www.fastcompany.com/1660088/
    twitter-rolls-out-places-adds-foursquare-and-gowalla-integration).

O'Dell, Jodie. "Foursquare's University Badges Now Available at All
    Colleges & Universities." Mashable.com, January 31, 2011.
    Retrieved March 2011 (http://mashable.com/2011/01/31/
    foursquare-colleges-universities).

O'Dell, Jodie. "Twitter Launches 'Places' Feature with Foursquare Integration."
    Mashable.com, June 14, 2010. Retrieved 2010 (http://mashable.
    com/2010/06/14/twitter-places).

Parr, Ben. "Foursquare and C-SPAN Team Up for Political Education."
    Mashable.com, June 22, 2010. Retrieved April 2011 (http://mashable
    .com/2010/06/22/foursquare-c-span).

Richmond, Shane. "Foursquare, Gowalla, and the Future of Geo-Location."
    Telegraph, March 11, 2010. Retrieved April 2011 (http://www.
    telegraph.co.uk/technology/news/7419847/Foursquare-Gowalla-
    and-the-future-of-geo-location.html).

Salt, Simon. Social Location Marketing: Outshining Your Competitors
    on Foursquare, Gowalla, Yelp, and Other Location Sharing Sites.
    Indianapolis, IN: Que Publishing, 2011.

Snow, Shane. "Foursquare vs. Gowalla: Location-Based Throwdown."
    Mashable.com, December 25, 2009. Retrieved March 2011 (http://
    mashable.com/2009/12/25/foursquare-gowalla).

Tabin, Herbert, and Craig Agranoff. Checked-In: How to Use Gowalla,
    Foursquare, and Other Geo-Location Applications for Fun and Profit.
    Deerfield Beach, FL: Pendant Publishing, 2010.

Van Grove, Jennifer. "Foursquare's Facebook Integration Now Live for iPhone
    Users." Mashable.com, December 18, 2009. Retrieved March 2011
    (http://mashable.com/2009/12/18/foursquare-facebook-2/).

Van Grove, Jennifer. "Foursquare: Why It Might Be the Next Twitter."
    Mashable.com, July 25, 2009. Retrieved March 2011 (http://
    mashable.com/2009/07/25/foursquare-app).

Wade, Katherine. "Foursquare for Universities Could Reward Check-Ins." Western Kentucky University *Herald*, April 26, 2011. Retrieved April 2011 (http://wkuherald.com/news/article_f1c41e26-6f9a-11e0-b07a-001a4bcf6878.html).

Wortham, Jenna. "Face-to-Face Socializing Starts with a Mobile Post." *New York Times*, October 19, 2009. Retrieved April 2011 (http://www.nytimes.com/2009/10/19/technology/internet/19foursquare.html).

Wortham, Jenna. "Foursquare Signs a Deal with Zagat." *New York Times*, February 9, 2010. Retrieved March 2011 (http://bits.blogs.nytimes.com/2010/02/09/foursquare-inks-a-deal-with-zagat).

INDEX

About the Author

Philip Wolny is a writer and editor living in New York. He has tried out various services such as Foursquare, Gowalla, and Facebook Places and remains continually astounded at the wide variety of online and real-time communities available to the digitally connected user.

Photo Credits